THE PITMAN'S POET

THE LIFE AND TIMES OF ARTHUR MORRIS

(1886 – 1929)

By G H Brearley FCMA

©2004 Giles Brearley
Typeset and Printed by Babash
The Shadowline Building
Wembey Street
Gainsborough
Lincs.
DN21 2AJ

This little book was a welcome surprise in my life.

I knew very little about my grandfather and when Giles Brearley first wrote to me, I was delighted to be furnished with so much information about Arthur Morris who, until then, had been a person of mystery to the whole family.

I was happy to fill in some details and, over the ensuing months, Giles and his researchers did incredible work.

Now, the "Pitman's Poet" has emerged from obscurity and has taken his place, not only in coal mining history, but also in the hearts of his relatives.

I do thank Mr Brearley and his colleagues for their tireless, brilliant and selfless research.

With appreciation and gratitude,

Julie Andrews

ACKNOWLEDGEMENTS

I am extremely grateful for Julie Andrews' assistance and provision of personal family material and to her assistant, Francine Taylor.

I would like to thank Ron James, our Swinton Heritage archivist, for the countless hours he has donated to the research into the life of Arthur Morris.

Thanks also to Durham Mining Museum, Yorkshire Mining Museum, Muriel Elliss of Wath, Walton on Thames Heritage Society, Ken Wyatt for assistance with the military information and Joanne Rayner for typesetting.

Information was extracted from the electoral rolls census, the 'South Yorkshire Times', the 'Sheffield Star', the Mines and Quarries Acts, as well as the never-ending resource of the Internet. Thanks to the donations of pictures and information from many members of the public.

I would also like to thank:-

The Laird of Camster for access to his large archive of printed books articles and pictures.

Mr A J Kear, assistant regimental archivist of the Grenadier Guards, Wellington Barracks, London.

John Gwatkin for information on Denaby.

Denise Hall, of Wolverton Society for Arts and Heritage for information and photo's.

Friends of Byfleet.

Conisborough and Denaby Main Heritage Society.

The Public Records Office, Kew.

The British Library.

Rotherham Archives.

Amy Brearley and George Legg for time spent in London on research.

Ruth Brearley for enthusiastically listening to the script being read so many times – she is now word perfect.

Members of the public in Hersham, who kindly offered information during my visits.

Assachar (Dick) Allport of Conisborough.

Tony Greathead.

To the many South Yorkshire residents who also loaned photographic material and recalled memories.

Introduction

I FIRST CAME ACROSS ARTHUR MORRIS when I stumbled on a couple of his poem sheets. I thought the standard of his poetry was exceptional. This, coupled with my own interest in the mining industry, which he portrayed, stimulated my desire to know more about him. I established that others had tried, in vain, to piece together the life of "The Pitman's Poet". I was convinced that the information was out there, somewhere.

The research was hard. My friend, Ron James helped, spending countless hours trawling through various archives. Although information was hard won, what little did turn up was astonishing and would lead us onto something else. The search for information even involved writing to Los Angeles in the USA. I undertook journeys to South London especially to try and go that "extra mile", wrote e-mails and letters to many people, societies and organisations. Ken Wyatt undertook some military research and started checking the various Local Authority records. With perseverance, more information was assembled to a point where I could at least pen a tribute to the celebrated "Pit Man's Poet". The ease at which you will be able to read about Arthur Morris is at least some thanks for the tireless efforts expended by us all. As his life history unfolded, the events uncovered were remarkable and tragic.

Not all of Arthur Morris' poems have been traced but hopefully as people wake up to his historical importance, more information may well turn up. If anyone does have further information, it will be gratefully received.

Please read on and marvel at this man's artistic talent and his achievements during the hard, economic climate of Victorian and Edwardian England.

G H BREARLEY

ARTHUR'S EARLY YEARS

AS GRACIOUS QUEEN VICTORIA was halfway through her forty-eighth year on the throne and while many of her subjects were busy propping up the vast empire that had been created during her reign, a young mother was about to give birth to a baby boy.

William Arthur Morris was born in January 1886. He had a unique birthmark in the centre of his back. He had blue eyes, brown hair and was of fair complexion. He was named after his father, William Arthur, who made his living at the time as a musician. His mother was called Alice and they resided at Wolverton in Buckinghamshire.

The London and Birmingham Railway Company founded Wolverton in 1838. The expanding railway network needed a stopping point midway between the two cities for refuelling and engineering facilities. As a result of the large number of passengers finding themselves in Wolverton, refreshment services and hostelries also developed. The Grand Junction Canal, which stretched from Derbyshire to London, also touched the town and great rivalry arose between the

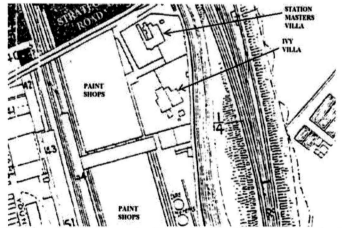

Map of part of railway works. Young Street, where the Morris family resided, is to the left hand side,
demonstrating its close proximity to the works.

companies for lucrative freight business.

Wolverton was Britain's first purpose built railway town, established on a green field site and attracted workers from all over the country as jobs were created. This phenomenon was duplicated over one hundred years later with the establishment of the neighbouring Milton Keynes. New homes were built by the Railway Company. Similar to Sir Titus Salt's Saltaire development in West Yorkshire, the Railway Company ensured that schools and leisure facilities were also incorporated into the new town's infrastructure.

The town itself was compact with red brick terraced houses, criss-crossed with wide service alleyways, acting as boundaries between the back gardens.

As the town developed, a keen sporting fraternity emerged. Competitions were held here for cycling, bowling and it also became host town to a national Victorian athletics event. By the time Arthur was 13, the town's football team was prospering, with a new wooden stand being erected and they were playing the likes of Chelsea and Tottenham.

Wolverton Railway Band

It is believed that William Arthur (senior) actually played for Wolverton Railway Band. This prize-winning brass band travelled up and down the country, performing in competitions as well as giving public performances. He also, more than likely, had regular playing venues to provide income.

There was a rumour in the family that William may not have been Arthur's father. His mother, Alice, had previously worked in service and "the skeleton in the cupboard" was that she had an affair with her employer and that Arthur was actually born on the wrong side of the sheets, a common occurrence in those days.

The London and North West Company School

Arthur attended the London and North Western Railway Company School, situated on Church Street. The company took it upon themselves to provide education for workers' families. The same building is currently used as the Wyvern Nursery School.

Arthur was noted as receiving a moderate education and achieved the Mid-Class 1st Certificate. He was an adventurous boy and gained a scar on his right groin from a childhood mishap.

He was brought up as a Wesleyan Methodist, attending the local chapel, which was also on Church Street.

As he grew into manhood, he attained the then considerable height of 5' 9½" and weighed 152lb with a 38" chest.

Arthur, in later life, used to relate to his daughters that his

The Weslyan Methodist on Church Street, where Arthur attended.

childhood was not altogether a happy one. He was often banished to the scullery for long periods mainly because his father could not stand the sight of him. This loathing may have been fuelled by the "skeleton in the cupboard" rumour. By 1901, the family had moved to 565 Young Street and life went on.

The numbering of the houses in Young Street was somewhat confusing as houses were allocated numbers consecutively as they were built. So number 564 could be somewhere in Birmingham and 566 in Crewe. Each property number was contained within an oval cast iron plate with "L.N.W.R." embossed onto it.

One regular feature of Arthur's life would have been the using of the town's Bath House, which was situated on nearby Stratford Row. It was also built by the Railway Company to serve the community. Many of the houses, including the "Little Streets" district, where Arthur lived, didn't have bathrooms. Whilst a thorough wash down was an every day routine at home, the Bath House was used to complete the

The old Bath House, Stratford Road.

buffing up to an overall cleanliness. With the large number of dirty jobs, the Bath House was in regular use. It remained in service as this right until the 1970's.

Arthur did not take up any of the many apprenticeships that were offered to the young men of the town, many being engineering based, but learnt how to cut hair and operated as a young barber.

The main Stratford Road through Wolverton
- known locally as "The Front"

The hairdressing trade was and still is notorious for the chitchat, which goes on with customers. Current affairs were always topical and there would have been much patter about the military crisis that was looming. Germany had commenced an arms building programme as the Kaiser prepared to increase his profile. The First Lord of the Admiralty, Reginald McKenna, revealed to all that our naval supremacy would soon be lost. Arthur must have had these discussions most days and perhaps, a spark was ignited.

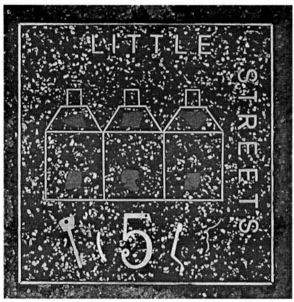

Waymarker in Wolverton today, depicting the area of the "little streets".

JOINING THE MILITARY

BRITAIN WAS STILL SMARTING from the effects of the Boer War in South Africa. This was, declared by the Boers on 11th October 1899 and had, in the words of Rudyard Kipling, given the British "no end of a lesson". The British Press made the most of the military success, such as the relief of the siege of Mafeking, which was the excuse for mass public celebrations, street parties and the like.

DAILY SKETCH.

THE ALL-PICTURE MORNING PAPER.

| Nº 1. | MONDAY, MARCH 15, 1909. | ONE HALFPENNY. |

TRANSPORTING A THOUSAND SOLDIERS IN MOTORS.

Headlines appeared in early 1909 with strong military content.

Military exhibitions were held to gain recruits

This triumphalism could not disguise the fact that the war proved to be the longest (2¾ years), the costliest (over £200 million), the bloodiest (at least 22000 British, 25000 Boer and 17000 African lives) and the most humiliating war that Britain had experienced. The Germans were heavily implicated in the Boer War, providing political support and arms to

Typical recruitment poster.

the Boer republics.

During much of the Victorian era, Russia had been seen as the major military threat to Britain's far flung empire. By the early years of the 20th Century, the young, strong, often-bombastic German Empire had become the new challenge with its growing naval power and mass conscripted armies.

Throughout Europe, alliances were being drawn up.

On 8th June 1909, Arthur travelled to Northampton and took the oath at the Wellingborough Barracks. He was recruit number 14385.

Arthur signed on as a volunteer in an army that was, at this period, enjoying peacetime soldiering. During the mid-Victorian period, a large programme of barrack building had been undertaken across Britain. The reason for this programme of public expenditure was twofold. Firstly, it was recognised that the health of the troops was greatly improved with decent accommodation, sanitation, protection from the elements and wholesome food. Many lessons had been learned from the experiences of the Crimean War when losses of troops from disease and neglect exceeded losses from combat.

The military authorities eventually adopted reforms advocated by people such as Florence Nightingale.

Secondly, it was recognised that the authorities to help quell civil disturbances could call upon troops dispersed in barracks around the country near population centres. Troops were called out to deal with political unrest and to help break strikes, often with fatal consequences for the workers. Between 1896 and 1908, troops had been called out on twenty-four occasions to aid the civil power.

Soldiers on guard at Caterham Barracks

Grenadier Guards in full dress.

Grenadier Guards at Caterham in 1910 - where is Arthur?

Arthur's first posting was to Caterham Barracks. Once he arrived there, politics would be the last thing on his mind. He would be disciplined and drilled in the style of the Guards. This was based on tradition, proven experience and knowledge of the human heart, under a regime, which would ensure that all recruits would advance the regimental honour. Their civilian habits and attitudes would be crushed and the men would be rebuilt as regular soldiers and guardsmen. Regimental officers and men had an extremely limited knowledge of what was going on outside their own particular corner. Their home and family became the regiment and a unique companionship was found among the men.

To be effective, an army must be well disciplined. From Roman times through to the Gulf Wars, it has been axiomatic that a well-disciplined force will invariably defeat one with poor discipline.

It was the job of the drill instructors and training staff under RSM Teech to turn sometimes-unpromising human material into guardsmen – the elite of the army at that time.

We know that Arthur was a sensitive and intelligent man with a good command of the English language. He would need to learn to keep his mouth shut, follow orders and rub along with the other recruits including, no doubt, drunken and licentious elements.

Training would include "square bashing" – drill movements carried out repeatedly until perfection was achieved and the drill sergeants were satisfied. Many hours would be spent

Caterham High Street - Ravaged by traffic today.

on "bulling" equipment to a mirror-like shine. Boots, buttons, brasses, webbing, rifles, etc, would have to be spotless on all sides. Any infringements would earn a fierce tongue lashing from NCO's who knew every obscenity there was to know. They could order a miscreant to do extra work, fatigues or even to spend time locked up in the guardroom.

One skill that was of prime importance to the British Infantry soldier was musketry. Fifteen aimed rounds of rifle fire per minute was the standard that most British regulars met. Extra pay was awarded to those who gained the Marksman's Badge. Much time would be spent on gymnastics to achieve a peak level in fitness. Arthur completed his military training and "passed out" a fully-fledged guardsman.

During this time, Regimental Sergeant Major Teech would have been the Barracks' "God". He would be the last person that Arthur or any of his fellow recruits would wish to cross. The RSM would have been avoided at all costs – men would have sought a hiding place on his approach. Teech would have been a life-long soldier, having most likely joined up as a boy. At the pinnacle of his army career, he would know every trick and excuse in the book and would tolerate none.

Any recruit would have felt his blood turn to water at the sound of Teech's stentorian voice bellowing. "That man there.

Double over here!"

No matter how immaculate a guardsman's appearance, Teech would be able to find faults. Buttons not polished front and back, traces of polish on uniform, a bearskin hat with hairs out of place, etc.

A dressing down from Teech would have been remembered until a man's dying day. He would have observed any bat of an eyelid, a movement of a pupil, the slightest facial twitch. All of these would have been difficult to avoid with RSM Teech's mouth half an inch from the recruit's eye, screaming with all the power of his lungs and extensive soldiers vocabulary.

Even the junior officers would have feared getting on the wrong side of the RSM. He would have been President of the Sergeant's Mess and when he entered, all the NCO's present (formidable men themselves) would have jumped to their feet and remained standing until they received "the nod".

The army was quick to recognise Arthur's civilian trade and appointed him to the barrack staff as camp barber. His duties would have included keeping the troops' heads nearly shaved bare – not only for smartness but also to keep down the threat of lice that would have been ever present. Arthur would no doubt have used the cutthroat razor to provide a daily shave especially to the camp officers and senior NCO's.

Had it not been for Arthur's trade, completion of basic training could have seen him posted early to a battalion that was serving overseas. Most army regiments had a battalion serving in some part of the Empire, often India, whilst the other battalion was stationed in Britain. These would rotate after a period of time. Had Arthur received an overseas posting, our story might have turned out quite differently.

Private time would often see the troops frequenting the inns and taverns of the local towns and on one such occasion, Arthur met a local girl, Julia Mary Ward who was aged 22 and working as a domestic servant. She was the daughter of William Henry Ward, who was working as a gardener. She lived with her parents, her brother and four other sisters – Fen, Dottie, Kath and Mena.

The family lived at 3 Rydons Grove, Hersham, Walton on Thames. This remained the Ward family home for many years. Herhsam was a pleasant town with a long history, situated on the River Mole. Many new buildings had been erected in its transition from a village. It was about 18 miles South West of London.

Arthur started seeing Julia at every opportunity and their relationship flourished. Arthur must have been extremely content with his military life as on 10th January 1910, he took the option to extend his military service to 7 years, which would have brought him a few more benefits. It was just after this time that Julia discovered she was expecting a child and some heated family meetings must have occurred. Arthur decided to do the honourable thing and married Julia on 28th February 1910 at the Registry Office, Godstone.

The marriage was witnessed by two of their friends, Mr W Harden-Bennett and Mr W George Avey. It was noted that at the time of the marriage, Julia's address was shown as Allistree, Caterham Valley. She had obviously moved out of the family home to be nearer Arthur.

There couldn't have been much of a honeymoon enjoyed, for less than one week later Arthur was back in the barracks. He had impressed his Commanding Officer so much that on 3rd March 1910, he received his first promotion, to Lance Corporal.

It was evident that Arthur came under a lot of pressure and his new wife probably didn't fancy being a soldier's wife and the situation between them must have been extremely tense. A soldier's hours were not 9.00am to 5.00pm, with weekends at home. The hours could be long and the days consecutive. Julia doted on Arthur and would have missed him greatly.

On 25th July 1910, Barbara Ward-Morris was born. There was possibly a conflict between what time Julia wanted Arthur to have off from the military compared to what the

Arthur Morris with wife Julia and their daughter Barbara.

newly promoted Lance Corporal could have off because on 30th July 1910, five days after daughter Barbara was born, Arthur did the unthinkable; he deserted his regiment. He was recorded as being Absent Without Leave after having served fourteen months.

It is not believed that Arthur travelled very far following his desertion and that he stayed in the district.

On 29th August 1910, Barbara's birth was registered by Julia at the Chertsey sub-district Registry Office at Walton on

A curious policeman ended Arthur's freedom - it may have been a relief.

Thames. After that, they seemed to disappear into thin air. The residential address given is back at the family home, which may be where they went after leaving Caterham Valley.

It was and still is normal practice that, the Army inform the civil police of deserter's details. They would ensure that both the local police and police in the soldier's hometown were alerted. Nothing was heard of Arthur and Julia until, on Bonfire Night, 5th November 1912, Arthur was asked to produce his ID by a curious policeman. A quick check established that Arthur was on the Army's "missing list" and was formally arrested and interned in the police station. Two days later on 7th November 1912, Adjutant, E A Ridley of the 2nd Battalion of the Grenadier Guards, arranged for him to be collected and taken into Army custody, pending court martial.

Arthur's prospects at this time would be looking quite bleak. He had let down his regiment, removed Army property without permission and breached "good order and discipline" regulations.

Arthur would have been taken from civilian Police custody by the Military Police. As a deserter, he would find little sympathy and would be facing a term of detention, either in the Garrison's Provost Prison or in the Aldershot "Glasshouse". Neither option would be a bed of roses;

punishment was the order of the day.

On 15th November 1912, he was tried and convicted and sentenced to 63 days detention in military prison, for desertion. He was also fined 15 shillings 8½d on two counts; one, for the actual desertion and the other for losing, by neglect, his arms and equipment. On 18th November 1912, Arthur was transported back to Caterham Barracks, where he would serve out the rest of his sentence in the penal cells.

There must have been great emotional reasons why Arthur committed the cardinal sin and pleadings were made on his behalf for, on 4 December 1912 after only 29 days in prison, the Army agreed to release him and he was formally discharged from His Majesty's services. As hard as Army life was, they would recognise that Julia was a new wife with a young child and needed financial support. The discharge papers list Arthur's character as "bad". The discharge address was to the Ward family residence at 6 Sandown Villas, Hersham Road, Hersham, where Julia had probably returned to, being under great financial pressure.

Coal Mining Calls

During 1913, Arthur and Julia decided to start afresh. Arthur had decided to join that established group of close comrades and become part of the Kent coal mining community. It was certainly a long way removed from his Army days.

There was increasing pit sinking activity in Kent and jobs were being widely advertised.

Mining was classed as an essential service and it may have been that Arthur believed it would also guarantee that he wouldn't be whisked back into the military with what was clearly becoming the advent of the First World War. It also gave him a chance to start afresh and leave his past behind him.

The Kent coalfield was a latecomer compared to the long established coalmines of the North.

The continuation of coal seams of Northern France under the Channel into Kent had long been suspected and following borings in 1882 for a possible Channel Tunnel; it was duly discovered to be present in sufficient quantities to justify commercial mining.

The Shakespeare Colliery was sunk at the base of the

The Church at Adisham.

work. The coalmine was dissected into several areas on each seam. Each area was known as a "district". His work during the shift meant that he supervised the erection of roof supports, the removal of props from old districts, changing air currents where necessary, testing for gas and clearing away bad air and any falls of stone. The deputy answered to the colliery overman who in turn, answered to the under-manager or manager.

The Act also prevented boys or girls, under the age of 14 or women of any age, from working underground. It did however, allow surface work from the age of 13 but prevented working between 9.00pm and 5.00am. They could also only work up to 54 hours per week with no more than 10 hours in any one shift.

The job was one that carried great responsibility; men's lives were in the deputies' hands.

Moving to Denaby, South Yorkshire.

As the First World War was drawing to a close, Arthur, who had not been long qualified as a deputy, decided to leave the Kent coalfield and move his family to the lucrative deep mine coal extraction of South Yorkshire. The family upped sticks and moved to the pit village of Denaby Main, taking a house from the colliery company at 62 Warmsworth Street, Denaby. Denaby Main is 5.4 miles south east of Doncaster on the south bank of the River Don. It had a population of around 6000.

It may have been that initially Arthur came to Denaby alone. It is known in the family that he "deserted" his wife, eventually returning with gifts and was once again, a loving husband and father for a while. Both of Arthur's daughters used to speak of this. It happened at the birth of each of his daughters. The first absence was most likely connected to his army problems.

The colliery was sunk in 1863 and had taken over what was previously a hamlet. The company built a new model town

Denaby Main colliery.

A miner's wife doing her duties.

The colliery had seen it's fair share of strikes.

Part of the colliery's rail stock.

for the workers.

Two shafts were sunk approximately 40 yards apart. The down shaft was 14 feet in diameter and the upcast shaft, 13 feet 6 inches. The mine extended down to 422 yards deep to reach the 9 feet thick Barnsley bed seam. At the time, it was the deepest mine in Yorkshire. The share capital of the company at the time was £110400 and was operating at a profit.

Ventilation to the mine was by way of a 40-foot diameter fan, which was powered by a 30-inch horizontal steam engine. The advances in ventilation technology allowed the collieries to venture into deep mining.

Steam winders operated, winding coal, men and materials up and down the shaft and five screens were built for coal separation.

The colliery was no stranger to controversy having been involved in the notorious "Bag Muck" strike of 1902/03, which saw the colliery company forcibly evicting people from the company's houses following a trade dispute. Over the years, there had been many strikes and fatalities. The sister colliery of Cadeby had been the site of the notorious "Cadeby Colliery Explosion", which saw 91 men killed in 1912.

At the time of Arthur's arrival, over 3500 men were working at the colliery. The other seams of the Parkgate, Hague Moor and Silkstone were also mined during the collieries life.

The colliery was kept under the watchful eye of the long-serving colliery manager, W H Chambers. He

WH Chambers,
King of Denaby

34

The Officials Cub, Denaby.

Young pony driver at work.

Miners hewing coal.

Pony pulling tubs.

was known as the "King of Denaby". He was not only a skilful manager; he had the welfare of his miners at heart and helped organise, promote and support many social and beneficial causes.

Denaby was certainly a lively town. In 1899, the Christian Bulletin described Denaby as the worst village in England although its strong community spirit prevailed. It certainly knew hard times and created hard people but it also created an immensely strong community spirit.

The house where the Morris' lived had two room upstairs and two rooms downstairs. Outside was a large rear yard with an outside toilet and coalhouse.

The houses were built in eight blocks of ten and constructed between 1902 and 1909. So when the Morris' moved, the house would have been relatively new. Gas, which was a waste product from the mining operation, was used as fuel in the houses and was first utilised in the village in 1898. Water was not laid on in the houses on Warmsworth Street until 1902 and electricity was not installed until 1953.

As a deputy, his standard of living would be quite high in comparison to his fellow mineworkers whom he directed. He would be looked up to and the fact that he was an outsider coming in meant he carried no personal baggage, which could have hindered him. The deputies had their own social club with membership restricted to their hierarchy so they didn't necessarily have to drink with the men. It was often said that more coal was "got up" here than at the pit itself! Their house was situated quite close to the colliery so Arthur could be at work in minutes.

Arthur, as a deputy, felt he was a notch above most of the others. Although Joan was not ready for school, Barbara was. He didn't fancy putting her with the rest of Denaby's children into the small array of schools that existed; he wanted something more special for his daughter. He found the answer to this by enrolling her at "Miss Allports Preparatory School for Boys and Girls" in the Old Hall, situated a little

𝕻reparatory 𝕾chool

FOR

BOYS AND GIRLS.

Miss ALLPORT,

The Old Hall, Church Street, Conisborough.

TERMS ON APPLICATION.

Advert for Miss Allport's School, where Barbara was placed.

Miss Allport's Preparatory School at Conisborough is now a restaurant.

over a mile away in neighbouring Conisbrough. The same building is today occupied by a restaurant.

For a weekly fee, Barbara was educated with a small number of other children, all put there by paying parents. It was akin to the modern day practice of many middle class families of sending their children to private schools. Although modest, it helped put the stamp of "We are different" onto a mundane background. Arthur always wanted to be seen as one step higher.

Barbara actually stayed at Miss Allports until Christmas. By this time, it was decided that Joan also had to start her schooling proper and so Arthur elected to enrol them in the village school at Old Denaby. Old Denaby was an old farming village, situated approximately a mile and a quarter from the mining town of Denaby. This move continued his previous trait of elitism.

Barbara is admission number 6003 and Joan, 6014 in the pupil information register. Their father is listed as William Arthur Morris – Deputy. It put that special ring to it! Other children in the register simply had their parents name.

Around five pupils made the daily trek back and forth. In summer, a shortcut could be taken through the woods and over the fields.

The Church of England School was presided over by Mrs Bayes, who was more than just a headmistress; she used to organise all sorts of outings for her pupils and also, put school concerts on and arrange garden parties.

Assachar Allport (Dick) recalls that Barbara was very talented and Mrs Bayes always used to let her play the piano. He said Barbara was very popular at school and very attractive and always turned the heads of the young lads as they were passing by and they couldn't keep their eyes off her!

Her younger sister Joan was quite different from Barbara, more reserved and not as forceful as her older sister.

Twice a year, the school would put on a show and there

The Old Church School.

would be a performance at the school for parents and then at the Parish Hall at the nearby town of Mexborough, where the Hall would be packed with the Vicar and numerous local parishioners.

Dick recalls that the sisters, even though very young, took the shows very seriously and strived for perfection. Indeed, in the show "Alice in Wonderland", Joan took the part of Alice and he of The Mad Hatter and they sang a duet together starting with the words "Now I found you amongst the roses".

Life at the school was very happy.

In Denaby, sport was well represented with an active football club playing at the Tickhill Square ground. There was a history of strong cricket teams as well as a bowling club.

One must not lose sight however that the effects of World War one were still being felt and many activities had to be put on hold for the time being.

Arthur was quickly accepted by the Denaby mining community, as colliery workers were imported from all over

Britain, his different accent would not have caused comment. There were Geordies, Scots, Welsh and Irish by the score.

It was whilst he resided at Denaby that he started composing and publishing his poetry, relating the lives and experiences of his colleagues. He composed:-

Ten Million Quid
Let's Have Some Coal Out
Datellers
Drowned in the National Pool
The Datem Line
Life Down a Coal Mine
The Minder or Coal
Death of a Buttie

and what is considered to be a classical piece in August 1921:

A Pit Pony's Memory of the Strike.

His poems were well received and he was dubbed the "Pitman's Poet".

Dick Allport can recall seeing Arthur, going door to door around Denaby selling his poems. He recalls he used to wear a large black cloak whilst he was doing this and looked like one of the old time actors from the silent movies. As you never saw anyone wearing such a cloak around Denaby, the children found his sight intimidating.

Arthur became very fond and respectful of the pit ponies. They were often worked hard and were known for their intelligence. They knew their pony drivers and a relationship would ensue. If the pony detected some animosity from a driver, his behaviour would reflect this but would alter at a

Cadeby Colliery disaster, 1912.

shift change with a different driver. As a miner, Arthur had to work with ponies and he still controlled them in his role as a deputy.

Some ponies had very strong characters and could be as militant as the men. They were also renowned for sensing danger and often saved a man's life. They spent their working lives in the dark and dust filled mines and never saw daylight other than on the annual holiday close down. The sight of pit ponies frolicking in the fields at other times meant that there was yet another industrial dispute. Interestingly, many of these ponies were imported from Russia.

Arthur used his musical skills to entertain. He started to build up his reputation and become increasingly in demand. Proud of his coal mining roots, his act often played upon this.

He got involved in Denaby Village life and was often praised for his charitable nature and support. He liked sport and appeared in and organised local events. He was a founder member of the "Royal Antediluvian Order of Buffaloes" and became "Brother Arthur Morris". The "Buffs", as they were affectionately known, supported the pursuit of brotherhood based on family principles.

For acceptance to a lodge, you have to convince the

Drinkers posing outside the Reresby Arms.

42

A Buffalo's meeting at Denaby.

members that you are a loyal citizen and genuinely desirous of taking part in the organisation and to do whatever is required to meet the needs of the less fortunate brothers and their families. The origins of the organisation go back to 1822. It was clearly evident that more and more demands for his services were being made.

On a Monday night on 19th October 1919 at the Reresby Arms Public House, the Lodge was formed under the "Grand Surrey" banner. This may have been coincidental but as Arthur had a wife from Surrey and spent a lot of time down there, there could be some connection. Sir Enoch David of the Order presided and seven members were inducted.

On 14th February 1920 at the same venue, a fundraiser was held, presided over by Herbert W Smith (Miners Leader) and the entertainment was partly provided by Arthur. The function was to raise funds to buy regalia

In 1920 alone he was also credited with:-

5th March 1920

Assisting the Denaby and Cadeby Cricket Club with a fund raising concert. He appeared with other local artists involving Horace Hillerby of Mexborough, E Berry, W Popple,

W Widdowson, H Havenhand, T Oldfield and The Mexborough Glee Party. Horace Hillerby had been appearing in local productions since 1891. He was associated with the Mexborough Hippodrome Theatre.

3rd April 1920

Co-organising a well attended concert at the large hall in Denaby Main to assist the Denaby and Cadeby Cricket Club and the Tennis and Bowls Club for funding alterations to the sports ground. Arthur appeared on stage himself and recruited co-artists who he knew to take part in the show. They included Miss Lily Jackson (soprano), Miss E Rothery (soprano), Mr Willoughby England (violinist), Mr G Williams (bass), Mr H Stowell and the Mexborough Excelsior Quartet along with the Denaby Ambulance Band and Accompanists, Miss Williams and Mr Stanley Walker.

Horace Hillerby, a local performer who assisted Arthur in some of his fund-raising shows.

27th November 1920

Appeared at a smoking concert held in the ambulance headquarters for fund raising along with I L Mosley, F Widdowson, W Widdowson and an instrumental quartet. Smoking concerts were often attended by men only. The attendees would be smartly dressed and smoke a variety of fancy cigarettes and cigars throughout the course of the evening, no doubt washed

*Arthur Morris
dressed to entertain.*

down with ale. It was the men's night of relaxation.

11ᵗʰ December 1920

Appeared in a musical evening for the Denaby and Cadeby Cricket and Athletic Club held at the Denaby Main Hotel. Other performers included A E Berry, W Widdowson, E Cresswell, F Wheatley and J Bucknall. Mr E Wigley was the accompanist.

By March of 1921, there were one million people unemployed. The coal owners were demanding a 50% pay cut. The Miners' Union refused to agree to this drastic request so the colliery owners locked the men out. A crisis quickly developed and the Government called a state of emergency and drafted troops into the coalfield areas. Coal rationing was also introduced.

On 16ᵗʰ June 1921, pit pony races were organised at Darfield in aid of the Animals Distress Fund, commencing at 5.00pm. The races held were:-

*The Snape Hill Stakes
Highfield Handicap
Low Valley Selling Plate
Darfield St Ledger and
Pit Pony Derby.*

The Derby winner was "Doctor" from Dearne Valley Colliery.

Arthur was moved by the events of 1921 and his poem, "Pit

Pony's Memory of the Strike" epitomises the year's events and the pit pony race itself, from the pony's viewpoint. He tells the story of the pony that won the Darfield "St Ledger" so named after the famous Doncaster St Ledger horse race, which took place only some 10 miles away.

Herbert Smith (The Man in the Cap), the charismatic Yorkshire miners' leader, was mentioned within Arthur's poem. He was born in 1862 in the Workhouse and started work down the mine aged 10. From 1906 to 1938 (the year

Poster - pit poney races.

he died), he was president of the Yorkshire Miners Association. When Stanley Baldwin asked him to allow increased working times and a cut in hourly rates, he simply replied "nowt doing". Described as wearing a cap the size of a large dustbin lid and a watch the size of a small dustbin lid, he was well known for his outspoken but honest views. He was very well respected. He took meetings at the village and also undertook certain civic duties. Also mentioned in the poem is Frank Hodges, the

Herbert Smith, the miners' leader. Arthur met him many times and included him in his poems.

HM King George V.

Viscount Lascelles of Leeds.

HRH Princess Mary.

General Secretary of the Miners Federation of Great Britain.

Arthur used to perform his poems in song and as monologues aided by a pianist. His reputation soon began to spread. Of his portfolio of poetry, "A Pit Pony's Memory of the Strike" and "COAL" were sent by admirers to the country's elite. His poems were acknowledged by:-

HM King George V
HRH Princess Mary
Viscount Lascelles of Leeds
HM Queen Alexandra
Lord Derby
Earl Fitzwilliam

He became known as the celebrated colliery "Deputy Artist". Many of his poems were printed onto sheets and sold to help alleviate distress in the mining community. He would always rally to assist a good cause as was evident by his many concerts.

As Barbara grew up, she was encouraged to master the piano, like her father.

HM Queen Alexandra.   *Earl Fitzwilliam.*

Joan, Arthur's youngest daughter, recalls "When Barbara was old enough, our father started to teach her to play the piano, which proved to be a tempestuous occupation for all of us. Temperamentally, they were very much alike, being both self willed and used to getting their own way. Many a shouting match was heard culminating with the sound of a sharp slap of a "box on the ear". He was probably instrumental in teaching her, but Barbara also had private lessons and built up her own piano skills to a very high standard. It was announced on 24th July 1920 that, at aged 10, Barbara had passed her first class primary section of the London College of Music. Her father is referred to as Mr Arthur Morris, the well-known entertainer.

On the 8th March 1921 at the Reresby Arms, the Reresby Pride Lodge meeting was presided over by Knight Enoch Davies. Entertainment was provided by way of the members of the "Cabaret Nights", which was appearing at the Mexborough Hippodrome. Arthur commended the artists for their professionalism. One thing was certain; Arthur was watching them, not just for entertainment value but also to study their act and style.

Arthur took part in his last concert in Denaby Main on 12th November 1921. This was at the Comrades Club. The Club was newly formed by Comrades of the Great 1914-1918 War. The concert was performed by the Reresby Pride Lodge of the Royal Ancient Order of Buffaloes Entertainers, organised by Brother Arthur Morris. Arthur organised the entertainment, which included:-

Knight Carlisle Smith, Primo Avonhand, Primo George Anley, Brothers Ted Richie, N Davis, Harry Wilson, Robinson and S Rose.

Proceeds from the concert were donated to the Comrade's Children's Outing Fund, which had been formed. As a result of the extreme times, it was decided that the children of members should at least have a summer outing next year. This concept still continues in today's Club, but is something simply taken for granted as yet another entry in the social calendar.

Arthur Moves to Swinton

Towards the end of 1921, Arthur had left his much loved Denaby Colliery and moved to 16 Temperance Street, Swinton. The reason for his sudden departure is still shrouded in mystery.

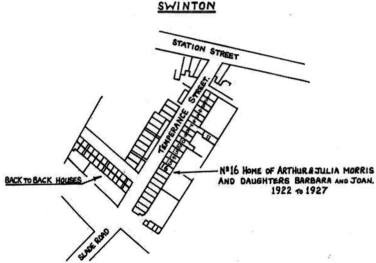

Map showing location of Arthur's house in Swinton (by Ron James).

Perhaps the move was seen as a breakaway from the strict mining environment of Denaby, to bring his daughters into a different environment and to further what he really enjoyed – being a performer. This is the most likely as if he was to launch as a professional entertainer, he could not keep his colliery house. If you did not work for the mining company, you came out! He always clung to his mining background; it had become part of him.

Swinton had been home to the world famous Rockingham

Looking up Temperance Street from Slade Road.
Arthur's house was halfway up on the right hand side.

Pottery. Although only a few miles from Denaby, it was much removed from the mining-dominated Denaby community. A small colliery struggled to operate at the top end of the town and other industries created employment, such as mineral water manufacture, the glass industry and iron founding. The town had two railway stations and was connected by them to Rotherham for onward travel to Sheffield making communications easier. The town had many fine buildings dating from the 16th, 17th and 18th centuries and comprehensive public amenities. Swinton had a population of around 12,000 and therefore, was quite large at the time.

Station Street, Swinton c1905.
Temperance Street was just off to the right.

Temperance Street was a Victorian built parade made up of terraced houses near the town centre. Arthur managed to find rented accommodation here.

At the time of the move, Arthur was aged 35, his wife Julia aged 32 and Barbara aged 12, whilst Joan was 6 years old. One big consideration was the continuing of the girls' education. They must have protested strongly, not wanting to leave their beloved Old Denaby Village School, where they were settled. It was decided that although an inconvenience, they could remain and would undertake the more arduous daily journey.

Each weekday morning would see them board a trackless at the Queen Street stop and alight some 2 ¼ miles away onto Doncaster Road at Mexborough. They then walked down onto Church Street, over the River Don via the ferry crossing, then a march up into Old Denaby up to the school. On alighting from the trackless in Mexborough, the walk was some three quarters of a mile.

Daughter Joan recalls her father at this time as being tall, of good countenance and upright, brainy with an elegant and at times, arrogant personality. If he desired he could be a great charmer.

Swinton was well connected for transport.

52

As Arthur's reputation spread, local criminals saw an opportunity to benefit from easy fraud, by printing and selling pirate copies of his poems. Arthur made the following statement in 1922:-

"I wish to inform the public that several men have been "duplicating" my "Poems" and are going from door to door selling "Pirate" copies of them. On the 9th March 1922, a Warrant was issued by the Alfreton (Derbyshire) Police for the arrest of a man who had travelled through Yorkshire, Notts and Derbyshire and sold thousands of copies of my poem entitled "A Pit Pony's Memory of the Strike". He also stated in some cases that he was authorised by me to sell them.

This is entirely a falsehood, as I employ NO agents. All my "Poems" are Copyright and fully protected and are entirely my own composition and property and every one has my own Photograph (as above) on the front of it.

Should any impostor call and offer you any of my "Poems" for sale, will you kindly inform the Police and oblige."

Yours very gratefully
ARTHUR MORRIS

This statement shows how Arthur's talents were appreciated by the mining communities and how far he travelled with his performances.

Whilst he was at Swinton he composed :-

The Miner's ABC, Life and Adventures of a Pit Pony and Wembley Colliery.

He was getting increasingly busy with his poetry, music and entertaining his young daughters with anecdotes. Barbara became an accomplished pianist at a very young age and now started accompanying her father on his stage tours.

On 1st August 1924 at the age of 14, Barbara left school. This caused more controversy as it meant that Joan, at age 9 years, would have to undergo the journey to Old Denaby alone or

Queen Street School, to which Joan was moved.

be taken to and from school. After protests from Joan to remain at Old Denaby, the Morris's decided to try and run with it. It must have caused some strain and difficulty as on 9th April 1925, Joan was taken out of school and transferred to nearby Queen Street, only five minutes walk from their house.

After leaving the old Denaby school, Barbara kept her association alive by acting as accompanist on the piano for the annual shows the school put on.

Barbara continued her playing progress and on 8th January 1926, it was announced she had passed the senior level exam in pianoforte' at the London College of Music, gaining a full diploma. She was tutored for this by Miss Hatton of Alexandra Road, Mexborough. It goes on to state "She is gaining a wide reputation as a pianist and has already played at many provincial concerts, including the Town Hall in Retford, Mansfield, Ilkeston, Wakefield, Chesterfield, Clowne, Doncaster and Nottingham. She has also broadcast on two occasions from the Sheffield studio of the British Broadcasting Corporation".

Barbara also taught music herself for the Royal College of Music Exams. In 1926, she is credited with successfully teaching:-

Intermediate Section –	Eva Russell
Elementary Section –	Olive Sybil-Williams
	Joan Morris (sister)
	Marion Towning
Primary Section –	Ronald Ward.

While all this was going off, Arthur's performances took him all over Yorkshire, Derbyshire, Nottinghamshire and Lincolnshire, playing to club audiences.

Arthur Morris – Notes by his daughter, Joan Morris.

"He excelled at piano playing and as a child; I thrilled to his skill as I watched him woo his audience. He always began with Old Comrades March – very quietly as though the band was afar off, the left hand keeping a steady 4/4 like the sound of marching feet.

Soon, he was playing the lovely counter melody on a great crescendo and everybody was foot tapping, eyes and faces bright with joy and the applause that followed the diminuendo as the band disappeared into the distance was proof in itself of his great ability.

He also had a ready wit and the gift of poetry, composing what, in those days, were risqué parodies to the latest songs, which he would render whilst accompanying himself on the piano. One of these was an old song called "Till We Meet Again" and I recall that when he was about to perform this, he would turn to our mother and say "Take the girls out for five minutes". Little did he realise that in the "ladies", we heard every word and although we didn't wholly understand, the implication was one of sex. It was about a recently widowed woman who was told that her husband's spirit would come to her if she sat naked on his grave at midnight. This was all cleverly explained in rhyme to the verse of the song – verses were very popular in those days, but the *piece de resistance* was the chorus, for she had inadvertently sat on a thistle in the dark, which tickled her and made her whisper (chorus):-

> *That's my old man!*
> *Oh it did give me a shock*
> *For he always was like this at twelve o'clock*
> *So come what might*
> *I'll be here every night*
> *'Til we meet again!*

It brought the house down!

After this epic, we were allowed to return in time for the encore, as follows:-

> *Two little boys on the path in the street*
> *Were arguing which had the dirtiest feet.*
> *They took off their stockings, their feet to compare*
> *The elder one cried, "I have won, I declare".*
> *Said the other "Sport, well you're five years older than me so*
> *you ought!"*

Then, one wonderful day, my father came home with a set of drums, which he learned to play while I watched, fascinated by the rhythms. When he thought he was proficient, he announced that he was going to hire the local church hall and, with my sister playing the piano and my mother at the entrance collecting the admission money, he began to run a series of profitable dances." (This was whilst they lived in Swinton, Mexborough.)

The hall Arthur used was the Parish Hall, which was situated on the main road through the town. Arthur would also compere and would have guest musicians to join him.

He excelled in his drum playing and he started doing performances. In September 1925, it was reported that the "Fragment Orchestra" had broadcast from Sheffield and included Miss Barbara Morris on the piano and Mr Arthur Morris on drums.

Barbara developed into a seasoned pianist in her own right. The South Yorkshire Times dated 8th January 1926, ran an article on Barbara confirming she had gained the diploma of "Associate of the London College of Music". It states she is gaining a wide reputation and had played in many provincial concerts and took part in two BBC broadcasts. It also confirms her sister, Joan, had just gained a first class in the elementary section of the piano.

WEMBLEY COLLIERY

AFTER THE DISASTERS left by the First World War, high unemployment and depression, King George V opened the British Empire Exhibition on 23rd April 1924. Its purpose was to stimulate trade and bond together the nations of the Empire, which covered almost every corner of the Globe.

It was held at Wembley and for 1 shilling and sixpence, you could gain admission to one of the greatest shows on Earth. It cost £10 million to fund the lavish exhibits. It included a palace of engineering, six and a half times the size of Trafalgar Square, a Taj Mahal replica, the Queen's dolls house, built one inch to the foot and a complete mansion. There was such demand to see it that it continued to open until October 1925. Some 17 million people visited in 1924 and another 9 million in 1925.

The Wembley Exhibition that so upset Arthur
and made him put pen to paper.

The exhibitions included a mock up of a colliery with pit ponies and the modern miners' home was also portrayed.

In 1925, Arthur, disgusted at how the exhibition misled the public as to how the miner's actually lived, penned a poem called "Wembley Colliery".

In the poem, he mocked the organisers for showing ponies that were not overloaded, no hot, wet places, no rats or mice, no strikes or grievances; just a model pit that never existed and therefore fooled the public by not showing the strife and hardship that went arm in arm with coal mining. He also paid tribute to the miners' wives for their roles.

In the poem, he refers to two disasters; the Cadeby Colliery disaster of 1912, when 91 men were killed after two explosions occurred, the second whilst the injured were being rescued. The nation felt for the community and their loss. King George V had attended Cadeby Colliery immediately after the disaster. He also referred to the Haig Colliery at Whitehaven, which was some 36 miles South West of Carlisle. Here, 39 miners were killed after firedamp was ignited following shot firing on the site in September 1922.

The Pitman's Poet felt so aggrieved, he had to have his say.

It is interesting to note that on the poem sheet that was distributed for the first time, he is referred to as "Late of the Grenadier Guards". Despite his misadventures during the his time in Guards, he was obviously proud to have served in the regiment, being not that long after the First World War, it brought respectability. It is also interesting to note that for the first time, he drops the reference to being "Late of Denaby Colliery". It was all part of his metamorphism into a more professional entertainer.

Arthur's Changing Times and Tragedy

Arthur's talents were certainly becoming more widely recognised.

Out of the deep, dark world of the coalmines, he had metamorphosed into a seasoned and talented performer.

Daughter Joan, in her notes, wrote:-

"My father was invited to many social gatherings and private functions. He was such a great entertainer and, of course, good looking and attractive to women.

My mother was hopelessly out of her depth and ill at ease in the more sophisticated company. As more and more invitations came in, my father went alone, his evenings out became more and more frequent and finally, my mother announced that we were going to Gran's in Walton on Thames. This was in 1927."

Barbara performed her last engagement on 5th February 1927, being pianist in a three night show, put on by the Swinton Players at the Church Hall. After the show was complete, Julia and her daughters left town.

Arthur remained in Swinton alone, furthering his cause but something dreadful started to affect him. He had contracted full-blown syphilis, which, in the 1920's, was still a major killer throughout the world. Indeed, it was suggested it could have been linked with the death of Winston Churchill's father and later; Al Capone became its most notorious victim. This social disease, mentioned by William Shakespeare, was about to claim another victim. In our modern times, this disease has once again become an increasing health problem.

Syphilis first appeared in the 16th century and has dogged mankind ever since. Its origins are strongly argued to be from the Eastern medicinal ointment containing mercury, to the importation from the new world by explorers and settlers.

The nature of the disease meant he could have contracted it quite some time before it became apparent, as it can lay dormant in the body for many years or it could have been contracted more recently.

Daughter Joan continues in her writings:-

"So life went on at Gran's. I thought of my dad frequently until one day, I came home from school and there he was. I think both parents benefited from the situation; my mother realising that she was unhappier without him than she was with him and perhaps he knew he was ill and returned to her loving care.

They were finally reunited but his vitality dwindled and he became thin and lethargic. He became so ill towards the end that he entered into the hospice care of the Brookwood Institute in Byfleet and finally died. My mother died a couple of years later."

Arthur may have been very fond of his wife and children but the new lifestyle that he had immersed himself in probably drove a barrier between them all.

Once on the circuit, he became increasingly popular and was invited to all sorts of venues and met a wide variety of people. The tall, handsome former pit deputy who had a talent for entertaining people would most certainly have appealed as a lover to many of the bored aristocratic ladies and female entertainers of the day. One thing for certain is that the "Pitman's Poet" let the wedge between him and his wife tempt him into a casual relationship with fatal consequences.

He must have been personally devastated knowing what he had done and how he had let Julia down. She obviously loved him greatly.

When Arthur first turned up at Julia's house in Walton, he was still well enough to work and he needed an income. Unfortunately, his coal mining skills would be of little use in Surrey and so he took on employment as a metal polisher for a local firm. He worked as long as he could but as his health worsened, he had to cease employment. Whilst at Hersham, he moved into the family home.

Thus, his address was again noted as being the Old Ward Residence of 6 Sandown Villas, Hersham, Walton on Thames. Arthur was admitted to the Brookwood Sanatorium, Woking, on 16th November 1928. This asylum had operated since 1867.

He was entry number 18218. He was without funds and was supported by the Chertsey Poor Union. He died on 31st August 1929 with the cause of death being given as "Paralysis of Insane". He was buried by friends; the end of a colourful life.

It appears that Julia had unfortunately been infected by Arthur and she started to become ill herself. She became an unwitting casualty to Arthur's forays, which was a great tragedy. Her death certificate states "Cause of death a) suppurative phyionephritis, b) cystitis, c) tabes dorsalis". So Arthur's philandering not only killed him but also took the life of his wife.

Life Continues

Arthur's eldest daughter, Barbara, continued her career as a pianist. She met a Ted Wells, who was a local handicrafts teacher in Walton on Thames and they married. They had two children, a daughter, Julia Elizabeth Wells who was born

Barbara Morris and her second husband, Ted Andrews. The familiar face of Julie Andrews is well reflected in her mother's features.

Early Promotional shot of Julie Andrews

on 1st October 1935 and a son, John David. Julia was named after both of her grandmothers.

Whilst Ted Wells was courting Barbara, he met Arthur and did not like him. He would take Barbara home after a date and be fearful for her safety. Arthur would have been in the late stages of syphilis and was drinking heavily. With his problems, he probably obtained some solace from the bottle.

The showbiz flair continued and at aged 2, Julia started lessons at a dance school, run by her Aunt Joan (Arthur's youngest daughter). In 1939, Barbara divorced Ted Wells and started a new life with Ted Andrews, a singer and vaudeville performer; they made up a double act. She had two more sons, Donald Edward and Christopher Stuart.

Ted discovered his stepdaughter had a magnificent voice and she was encouraged to take singing lessons from madam Lillian Stiles-Allen.

During 1944, she was performing in her mother and stepfather's touring show. Her surname was legally changed to Andrews and her first name changed to Julie. She went on to become the internationally acclaimed superstar, "Julie Andrews".

Joan Morris married Bill Wilby. They had a child, a boy named Jeffrey, who sadly died two weeks after birth.

Joan ran a dance school in Walton on Thames for over fifty years. She died on 28th February 1999.

Barbara sadly died in Chertsey, Surrey at St Peter's Hospital on 19th December 1984.

Would not Arthur Morris, the celebrated South Yorkshire colliery deputy, artist and pit man's poet, have been extremely proud of his daughter's and granddaughter's achievement?

Postscript

Plaque to Arthur Morris, which is situated on the corner of Temperance Street and Station Street in Swinton

THE END OF ARTHUR'S LIFE can only be described as a tragedy and that of Julia's an even greater travesty of justice.

With the benefit of hindsight, I am sure that events would have been completely different. Arthur was obviously a talented individual with a strong character backed up by a solid determination.

A saying that was common during Arthur's lifetime was that, "You are only four weeks away from the workhouse".

People had little or no savings and most homes were rented. The weekly income was needed to raise the family, put food on the table and pay the landlord off. If anything was left, it would be put aside for a rainy day, of which there were many.

Arthur's metamorphism from coal miner into seasoned entertainer dragged some of the mining culture and humour with

Unveiling the plaque

it. The times dictated it would be a long process as obtaining sufficient, personal, economic sustainability was difficult.

He was a hard taskmaster and expected a lot from his daughters, perhaps to a level where, at times, they were intimidated. He took a great interest in their cultural and artistic abilities. He had mixed with people who were the salt of the earth but, as is natural for most fathers, he tried to steer his daughters on to a higher plain that he had striven for.

Although Arthur's days ended prematurely, he had enjoyed a full and colourful life; perhaps it is only what you would have expected from "The Pitman's Poet".

A Selection of Arthur Morris' Poems

A "Pit Pony's" Memories of the Strike

Written, composed and sung by Arthur Morris

I'm only a pit pony and where I prove my worth,
Is where there is no "daylight" in the bowels of the earth?
But one day I can tell you I was filled with joy untold,
They took me to "pit bottom" and my eyes they did blindfold.
In the "cage" then up the "shaft", I seemed to go with pride,
The winder must have thought of me, 'twas such a gentle "ride";
At last I'm on the "surface" from the "cage" I'm led away,
They take the "cover" off my eyes; I see the light of day.
Later on my mates come up and then it came to pass,
They took us down into a field and turned us out to grass.
We held a meeting in that field, 'twas just beside a "dyke"
And we came to the conclusion that the pit must be on strike.
We thought of "Hodges" and "Herbert Smith"
       and then my mate called "Guss"
Sang, "They are jolly good fellows and so say all of us".
Then as we "jazzed" around that field, each pony thought that day
That he had found that "Happy Land" far, far, away.
One day our "boss" he came you know and made us feel forlorn,
We thought that we were going back
      where the "moggies" pinch our corn.
To our delight he took us amongst crowds and smiling faces,
Alas! This was our "Jubilee" the first "Pit Pony Races".
Now first I heard a tremendous noise, which made the people shift;
I said to myself there must be a "runner" down the "drift".
But as the noise grew nearer, 'twas "music" understand,
I fancied I was "Kissing Cup" as I marched behind the band.
Now one thing that annoyed me when they brought us ponies out,
A "bookie" looked at me you know and then began to shout,
"Two to one, bar one; I'll lay ten to one" you see,
While down the pit my "run" of tubs is limited to three.
I thought what does he take me for "ten to one I'll lay" said he,
Here's another one will lay down too if he puts ten tubs on me.

My jockey then he mounted, we paraded down the course;
I seemed to hear the people shout "My word, ain't he 'some' horse".
We then went to the starting post, all feeling quite sublime,
Where some chap with a little flag formed us into line.
My driver said "you've got to win, so do not disappoint",
I felt like asking him if he had changed his "Tommy Point".
At last "we're off" and scamper up the "course"
                                        by scores of "coppers";
"Oh Lord'" I thought, "what's coming off"
                                        my driver's "missed" his "lockers".
He digs his heels into me as on my back he's stooping,
And then I think, "What's up with him, is he afraid of "roofing".
Now as I galloped on and on, my driver seemed to say,
Go for all you're worth because there's no "muck" down today.
I made a special effort, my driver he sat tight,
But just two lengths ahead of me was a pony on my right.
We'd not much further now to go; I could see the winning post,
That pony still in front of me was what upset me the most.
My driver let me have my head then my best "form" I showed
As that pony seemed to "stumble" and get off of the "road".
'Twas over now, I'd passed the post the sun was shining bright;
I'd won and those who'd backed me were frantic with delight.
So when you talk of "Donoghue",
                                        "Humorist" and "Square Measure",
Please don't forget 'twas I who won the "Pit Pony St Ledger".
I've had thirteen weeks holiday; I have upon my soul,
And now I'm back down pit again, getting out some coal.
If ponies down pits could speak, with one accord they'd cry,
"If there could only be another strike,
                                        we'll let the rest of the World go by."

The Miner's ABC

by Arthur Morris

A
stand for "Airways", fresh air to us they give;
And though we're miles out underground, enable us to live.

B
stands for "Byeworkmen", the time they have its grand;
If "playing" in the "Football Team", "Cricket Team" or "Band".

C
for "Cutting Corner", where we always wish they'd "soften";
'Cause that is where the "coal" you know,
$\qquad\qquad\qquad\qquad$ wants hitting "hard" and "often".

D
stands for "District", where the "Deputy's" essential;
"Taking up" day, we always pray, he has a good sharp pencil.

E
is for "Explosions", which always draw attention;
"Whitehaven" and many more, too numerous to mention.

F
stands for "Flat Sheets", most "stalls" use "underground";
It's a "picture" when their "wetting" them
$\qquad\qquad\qquad\qquad$ to make the tubs "slew" round.

G
stands for "Gas", one of the miner's bitterest "foes";
It's claimed hundreds of "victims", as history plainly shows.

H
stands for "Haulage Hands", you've heard of them no doubt;
Usually on the "last ride" down and on the "first ride" out.

I
is for "Inspector", whom we very seldom see;
Except, of course, when there occurs a sad "fatality".

J
is for the "Jim Crow", on whose "cramp" we all depend;
In laying "turns" and "junctions", it's the "road layers" best friend.

K
is for the Kitchen", where our coal gives great assistance;
And we're handsomely rewarded by just a mere existence.

L
stands for "Lamp", "indispensable" to all;
It lights the way for us each day and "illuminates" our "stall".

M
is for the "Market Man", "up" and "down" he has to roam;
And if he's not "well-in" of course, he often goes back home.

N
stands for "Now't" or "Nothing" so to speak;
It's what you get for "lifting" your "ropps" out every week.

O
is for the "Overman", who's "chatty" with each man;
From "day-today", some people say, to get all the news he can.

P
stands for "Pit Pony", precious little pet;
Also for "Props" that are sometimes hard to get.

Q
stands for "Queue", you're in one every day;
To "get your lamp", "ride the rope" and also get your pay.

R
stands for "Ropeman", "Road layers" and "Rob Dogs" too;
Any "miner" will, no doubt, inform you what they do.

S
is for the "Sylvester", which every stall should keep;
It's used to get "back timber" out and some it puts to "sleep".

T
stands for "Tubs" with "dirt", "right full up to the brim";
'Tis when you get one "off the road" you sing "God save the King".

U
for "Undermanager", if your stall's an "abnormal treasure";
Just go to him to "make you up", he's happy beyond measure.

V
for "Ventilation", you'll find it's "sweet" and "clear";
That's if the next "stallmen" have had a "weekend on the beer".

W
for "Water", some men work in "underground";
It also stands for "Wind Up" when the "Inspector's coming round.

X
is for "'Xperience", thousands never had before;
When "anybody" worked in pits, while "miners" went to "war".

Y

stands for that "Yard Stick", a very similar sound;
And "Yardage" on your "Pay Sheet", which often can't be found.

Z

stands for "Zeal" so let us practice "lads" and "men";
That "Golden Rule" of "Safety First" and all reply "Amen"

THE LIFE AND ADVENTURES OF A PIT PONY

By Arthur Morris

"Life stories" of "Famous Men" are published far and wide,
And life stories of "Heroes" who for their country died.
My life story may interest you, as ever since my birth,
My life's been spent deep down below, in the "bowels" of the earth.

For years and years I've worked and done my duty faithfully,
And tried my very best to serve the Colliery Company.
But now my "working" days are "done",
        I'm "old" and "worn out" too,
So my adventures down the pit, I'll relate to you.

My home's near "pit bottom" as it's possible to be,
And when my "shift" is ended, that's the place I long to see.
But many times when I've reached home
       and "task's" been none too light,
They've fetched me out again before I've had a bite.

I've had all sorts of "drivers", some were very, very kind,
I've also had some drivers, the worst "brutes" you could find.
For instance, No 1 I had, he'd treat me like a "hog",
And if a tub got "off the road", he'd kick me with his "clog".

His orders were, my run of tubs was limited to "four",
But when there was no one about, he's "hung on" many more.
Sometimes he'd put on "twenty tubs",
       which made my legs fair "totter",
And if I could not "pull" them, he'd "bash" me with a "locker".

Driver No 2 I had, he was a pal to me,
He'd often bring a "carrot" or a "turnip" for my "tea".
A knob of sugar now and then when my "shift" was "complete",
And best of all, he'd always see that I was not "ILL TREATED".

He used to drive a mate of mine; old "Tony" was his name,
and "Tony" often told me that he served him just the same.
And when my mates at "weekends" had "extra" work to do,
They hoped the lad to fetch them out was Driver No 2.

One day, with colliers on the "face" for "water" he was "tapping",
It flooded out the "stalls" while I was in the passbye "snapping".
He "waded" thro waist deep to me, "released" and sent me "home",
And then was "carried" back again by the awful "raging foam".

Alas poor Driver No 2, he's in ETERNITY,
And what is more, I feel quite sure, he gave his "life" for me.
And when he gets to "Heaven's Gates", if the good old Bible's true,
The "King of King's" will say to him "PASS" Driver No 2.

Driver No 3 I had was very hard to please,
He'd never try to see that I was working at my "ease".
And when thro' "roofing" down a "gate"
                                   my "back" was rubbed "red raw",
He'd merely put some "tub grease"
                         and some "coal dust" on the "sore.

Driver No 4 I had, he was a "football" lad,
"Twas, "football" this and "football" that,
                              aye, he was "football" mad.
He'd backed 3 "homes" and 3 "aways",
                         won the "sweepstake"; I'll be bound,
And nearly got his "coupon" right to win £1000.

Each "run" on to "main level" he didn't half used to "chin",
And with the other "drivers", he'd be filling "coupons" in.
He'd then discuss the "sweepstake" held at several of the Clubs,
and then he'd tell the colliers that he'd had to wait for tubs.

I had a pal named "Jerry" once, who used to "run" and "drift",
He lost his life thro' "carelessness" whilst working out his "shift".
And when he passed me in a tub, he looked an "awful" wreck,
The "door trapper" had fell asleep and Jerry broke his neck.

I have some "happy" memories as well as sad ones too,
The "happiest" is that "13 weeks" from April 22.
The "Pit Ponies St Ledger", the "field" beside the "dyke",
I told you all about it in my "Memory of the Strike".

There's one thing that I really think the "public" ought to know,
That's how they treat us ponies, who work deep down below.
Our "miners" work one shift per day and what I fail to see,
Is why we sometimes work 2 shifts, very often 3.

They say that for the "coal" we draw
                             there's "royalties" for the "knobs",
The "royalties" we usually get are
                             "sticks" and "whips" and "clogs".
No doubt they feel quite flattered as they at their "mansions" gaze,
But scores of times I've never seen my "home" for several days.

We're only poor "dumb" animals, don't think I've got a cheek,
We cannot say when "tired" or "ill" because we cannot speak.
But all you drivers down the pit, a word I'll say to you,
Be kind and treat your pony as my Driver No 2.

There's one thing I should like to see, I'll tell you if I may,
And that's a "weekly" visit from the RSPCA.
A daily "record" of our work for Inspectors to survey,
Also to see we are not worked above an 8-hour day.

Another thing concerning us that I would recommend,
Is that we're brought up in our turns to "daylight" each weekend.
And now dear reader, will you help to let the country know,
There's "still" room for "improvement"
                             in our "treatment" down below.

*(All the "drivers" in this poem are fictitious
and do not refer to any living person or persons.)*

Wembley Colliery

By Arthur Morris

"If you have got time to spare, just for a tick or two,
A place called "Wembley Colliery" I'll introduce to you,
It has a 'reputation' and a "world wide recognition"
In London at a place they call the "Empire Exhibition"

This colliery was visited by thousands every day,
To see the 'miner' at his work, some millions they did pay,
They thought it simply "wonderful" as they glanced 'left' and 'right'
And many people wondered why the 'miners' ever 'strike'.

Yes everything was all-OK and also I may state,
That no one works in 'water' and it never is on 'weight',
There is no 'stalls' fenced off for gas or dirt to shift for 'now't'
And on each 'deputy's' report, it's 'true' what he has wrote.

The ponies they looked 'pictures', people gazed on them with pride;
What 'charming little creatures' was heard on every side.
They were not 'overloaded' or 'overworked' oh no,
Also they were not 'roofing' anywhere they had to go.

Delighted visitors all thought, this colliery was nice,
They were no hot wet places, also no 'rats' or 'mice',
'Fancy' no 'deputations', no men are 'victimised',
Also, no 'strikes' or 'grievances', and all are satisfied.

Crowds descended down this pit, who'd not seen one before,
The 'impression' that it gave them was a long way out, I'm sure,
In fact some people who about the 'miners' they had read,
Thought his quite a 'pleasant' task to earn his daily bread.

They'd also read of miners with their 'troubles' and their 'strife',
But judging from this 'model pit' he has a glorious 'life',
And if you ask a 'miner, what is 'Wembley' he will say
That is a 'happy pit' far, far away.

It's said that many men and lads, who down this pit did go,
Have come to the 'conclusion' that they'd like to work 'below',
My advice to all of them is whether 'young' or 'old',
Bear in mind the 'proverb' all that glitters in not gold.

The miners 'modern home' is there and what a pretty sight,
For there's a 'bathroom', 'hot and cold', also 'electric light';
Yes 'Wembley's', 'miners home' is grand, a cosy little 'nook'
But 'Colliery districts' that's where the 'public' wants to look.

Many, many people say they pay 'dear' for their coal.
But 'Whitehaven' and ' Cadeby Main' have paid a 'dearer' toll,
They sacrificed their 'lives' for 'coal', it's only too well know,
And those who do not sympathise deserve to get their own.

Then 'hats off' to our 'miners' all and 'hats off' to their 'wives,
They never know from day to day, ere they may 'lose' their 'lives'.
And do not think our 'collieries' are quite so 'danger free'
As the 'perfect', 'ideal' pit you've seen called Wembley Colliery.

An Earlier Attempt to Try and Research Arthur Morris

This letter, by well-known author, Jim MacFarlane, appeared in the 'South Yorkshire Times' on 3rd July 1976.

Julie's Grandfather!

Sir,-

A poem, "The Miner's ABC" by Arthur Morris, was published in pamphlet form sometime in the 1920s. Arthur Morris was the author of other coal mining poems including "The Miner or C-O-A-L" (graciously accepted by H M The King, HRH The Prince of Wales, HRH Princess Mary, H M Queen Alexandra, Lord Derby, Earl Fitzwilliam, etc), "Life Down a Coal Mine", "Death of the Buttie" and "Let's Have Some Coal Out".

In his published works, Morris went under the style of "The Celebrated Colliery 'Deputy' Artiste" (late of Denaby Main Colliery) and at the time of publishing the "ABC", he lived in Swinton near Rotherham. His poems appear to have been very popular in the coalfields of Yorkshire and the North Midlands.

When I first became interested in the poems of Arthur Morris – as a useful additional source on the social history of coal mining in Yorkshire – I attempted to trace further evidence of his work. Miss Judith Greenwood of Sheffield City Library was extremely helpful in checking local sources and checks were also made at other libraries in the South Yorkshire area without success. Enquiries at various national libraries drew a similarly bland response and although the word "copyright" is prominently displayed on the first page of the "ABC", there appears to be no record of Morris's work in the catalogue of the British Museum.

At one point in the research on Morris, having tried most of the formal sources of information without success, I was tempted to write what little seemed to be known about him and let the issue rest. I was saved from this faux pas by an impulse letter to the 'South Yorkshire Times', requesting information on Arthur Morris from local readers. The six or seven replies to the letter, from retired miners like Mr Ardron of Kilnhurst and Mr Jack Wilkinson of Brodsworth, a retired school-teacher, brought some surprise information. It appears that Arthur Morris, our coal-mining poet, had left the South Yorkshire area in the inter-war years. Sometime later, his daughter Barbara ("A very good piano player") married Ted Andrews, a "dance band leader". Later on, Ted and Barbara Andrews had a daughter, Julie and Arthur Morris, our "Celebrated Colliery 'Deputy' Artiste", author of "The Miner's ABC" had another grand claim to fame – as the grandfather of Julie Andrews, actress.

Yours, etc.
JIM MACFARLANE
The University of Sheffield
Dept. of Extramural Studies

(The letter is as printed but is a little erroneous.)

PIT TERMINOLOGY

Bookies Bookmaker who took bets on horse races, etc, from the miners.

Byeworkmen Workers who work away from the coalface. For example, a "dinter" who ensures a mine passage remains level or a tracklayer.

Cage Metal box of a rectangular shape, often two galleries, by which men and materials are lowered into or brought back out of the mine.

Capping The drawing off of water trapped in a seam to alleviate the risk of accidents when coal cutting takes place.

Clog Early wooden soled leather boot, later replaced with steel-toed safety footwear.

Colliers Coal face workers.

Coppers Police officers.

Datallers Underground labourers were paid a daily rate. Often included on first shift after a mine has been stood for a period of time to clean up falls of rock.

Districts Area of the mine, eg, S21's (Silkstone seam coal face number 21).

Door Trapper Operates a door on an underground roadway to assist ventilation. The job was often carried out by the youngest of the miners. He would open a door one way to let a pony, etc, through but then place it back for the airflow.

Drift Sloping passage connecting one level to another or down to a lower seam.

Drivers Pit pony operative.

Dyke Surface drainage to take water away.

Gate Underground roadway. (Main gate and Tail gate onto and off of the coal face.

Haulage Hand Men working on transport of materials around the mine.

Inspector H M Inspector of Mines appointed by the Government to ensure that legislative working conditions are adhered to. Prosecutions could be issued where breaches were found.

Jim Crow Tensioning tool used for bending metal.

Junction Where two or three different underground driveages meet up.

Locker Double meaning device to alter direction of a rail and also a lockable steel cabinet for personal effects.

Market Man Not part of a regular team but used to cover for peoples' absence in established teams of workers. Sometimes, gangs of market men were used together on a particular task when labour was short.

Moggies Cats.

Muck Impurity caught in between the layers of a coal seam can vary greatly in depth and number of bands.

National Pool Attempt to stabilise coal production and prices.

Nobs Gentry mine owners of the time.

Overman The most Senior Deputy, a Seam Overman would be in charge of all the deputies, shot firers and men on that seam.

Pit Bottom The area near to the shaft where ponies were often kept. Officials underground offices, etc were also here.

Props Logs or iron props bolted together, used to hold up the roof.

Ride the Rope This was an expression where miners used to obtain a lift on the mechanised rope haulage rather than walk.

Road Layer Underground worker who lays down track or base in an undergrounddriveage.

Rob Dogs Your fellows who cheated you.

Roofing Dual meaning. For pony drivers, it was an expression whereby the roof had come so low at some points that it caught the pony's back (roofed them). Also means the repair work being done to stop this.

Rope Man A specialised splicer who repairs the many cables and ropes used underground as well as

	dealing with their regular maintenance.
Ropps	Miner's expression to indicate he has had to work extremely hard – "He has worked his ropps off".
Royalties	An amount paid to a landowner for every ton of coal mined.
Runner	A runaway tub – extremely dangerous.
Shift	Three shift system – days (6am – 2pm), afters (2pm – 10pm) and nights (10pm to 6am)
Stallmen	Coal face workers extracting coal from a measured area (a stall). Also known as a "pog".
Sylvester	Aid for dragging out props or similar.
Tub	Coal carrier mounted on wheels, used to transport coal from the coal face as well as materials into the districts.
Under Manager	The Manager responsible for a seam and reports directly to the Colliery Manager. Seam Overmen would report to him.
Weight	An expression to indicate that serious pressure is being exerted on an area of the mine, usually after coal has been removed. The pressure from this can bend a prop double.
Yard Stick	Used to measure roadway advances or coal hewed out.